Other Books in the
Zondervan Series:

Taking Flight: The Katie Story

Breaking Through: The Bono Story

Cliff Hanger: The Don Nelson Story

Defender of Faith: The Mike Fisher Story

Gift of Peace: The Jimmy Carter Story

Driven by Faith

the
Trevor Bayne
Story

Godwin Kelly

ZONDERVAN.com/
AUTHORTRACKER
follow your favorite authors

It is true. You learn something every day of your life.
I was enriched and inspired by a wide-eyed,
twenty-year-old man as I researched and wrote this book.
And thanks for all your love and faith
Diane, Ellie, and Casey.
Time to walk the dogs again...

Table of Contents

Introduction

A personal note from Trevor Bayne

Thank you for reading *Driven by Faith*. The number one message I hope you get from reading this book is that God is powerful, and when we surrender and give him control, he'll take control in big ways and make big things happen. When we surrender control to God, he can do way more than what we could ever imagine, and that's what happened with me. I never would have dreamed in a million years some of the things that have happened to me were possible, but when I let God do it, they were possible.

— *Trevor*

Chapter 1

Two Laps to Glory

With two laps to go at the 2011 Daytona 500, Trevor Bayne found himself on the edge of victory. And it wasn't just because the turns at Daytona International Speedway are banked at an outrageous thirty-one degrees. The twenty-year-old rookie driver was actually in the lead!

Called the "Super Bowl of Stock Car Racing," the Daytona 500 kicks off the NASCAR season each February. A first-time driver winning Daytona is sort of like a college football team pulling off an upset in the National Football League's Super Bowl. It's unimaginable.

But the 2011 Daytona 500 had already proven to be full of surprises. The track had recently been repaved, which increased the speeds and led to a new style of racing. During practice races leading up to Sunday, drivers discovered a new style of racing known as "tandem racing," which put two cars bumper-to-bumper, traveling at nearly 200 miles per hour.

"Looks pretty easy doesn't it?" one of the TV announcers joked early in the race. "Think you could drive a car, folks at home, at 200 miles an hour with somebody pushing you?"

The close confines had already gotten the best of extremely experienced drivers. A major crash less than thirty laps into the race had eliminated many of racing's top names from contention, including Jimmie Johnson, Jeff Gordon, Matt Kenseth, and Michael Waltrip.

Early in the week at Daytona, Bayne found he was best suited as the "push car." So on race day, he felt very comfortable in the role of assisting more well-known drivers to the front of the pack.

By the time Bayne found himself in front, the two hundred lap competition had already seen seventy-four lead changes — a record! Twenty-two different drivers had led in the race, which had also seen a record number of caution flags with sixteen.

With accidents and blown engines happening all around him, Bayne had remained calm behind the wheel of the number 21 Wood Brothers Racing Ford and stuck to the game plan. That plan was to "push" his teammate David Ragan in the number 6 Roush Fenway Racing Ford to the front.

The pair had formulated that plan while following the pace car during a yellow caution flag (see "Flag Formula") in overtime of the race. The Daytona 500 is always scheduled for two hundred laps around the 2.5 mile course. But a caution flag in the final miles of the race forced extra laps. When a late-race caution keeps an event from ending under a green flag, NASCAR allows for up to three restarts so drivers can finish trying to pass each other all the way to the checkered flag. As the field rounded turn four behind the pace car, they were completing lap 202. There would be at least two or more laps to decide the champion in "The Great American Race."

Everything was on the line. Not only would the winner be added to an elite group of Daytona 500 champions, but he would also receive a large chunk of nearly $1.5 million in prize money. Neither Bayne nor Ragan was thinking about the paycheck. Both were focused on winning the race. When the green flag was shown to tell drivers to resume racing, Ragan planned to slip in front of Bayne, who had agreed to push Ragan's stock car ahead of the competition. Once the drivers had separated themselves from the pack, they would decide the race between themselves.

Eager to join forces with Bayne, Ragan pulled in front of Bayne's car before reaching the start-finish line. NASCAR's officials, watching from a tower above, waved the black flag at Ragan for "jumping the start."

According to NASCAR rules, Ragan had to give up his prime position, pull into the pit area, and return to the track at the back of the field. With Ragan gone, Bayne was now the leader of the Daytona 500 in only his second start in NASCAR's marquee Sprint Cup Series.

David Ragan (6) crosses the start/finish line in front of Trevor Bayne (21) and Tony Stewart (14) during a restart in the Daytona 500 at Daytona International Speedway in Daytona Beach, Florida, on Sunday, February 20, 2011.

The driver, who was a mere teenager two days before, now realized he was in control of the race with 182,000 spectators packed into Daytona and millions more watching on live television.

"That was the first time during the whole race that I really felt panicked," Bayne told the media the next morning. "I was like (over the two-way radio system), 'Guys, do I let Tony Stewart get in front of me and just push him? Do I back up? What's going to happen?' So I'm coming to the green, and I'm still on the mic saying, 'What should I do?'"

Crew Chief Donnie Wingo said, "Just go with the 47!" Bayne's natural racing instincts took control of the number 21 Ford. Bayne may have been new to the Sprint Cup Series, but he wasn't new to racing. He'd been driving racecars since he was five. He had led and won hundreds of races. This was a big stage, but it only required a basic racing strategy—go fast, stay in front.

Of course, with NASCAR's best drivers on your bumper, that's easier said than done.

When the green flag came down, NASCAR veteran Bobby Labonte in number 47 got a great restart. He was on Bayne's tail in no time as the pair rocketed to the front. Just as quickly as Bayne and Labonte created the gap, it was closed by Kurt Busch and Juan Pablo Montoya—who were just inches behind Labonte as the white flag waved to signal that just one lap remained.

Many great races at Daytona have been decided in the final lap, and this was gearing up to be a spectacular finish.

Heading into the last turn, Carl Edwards and David Gilliland looked like they were shot out of a cannon as they went low on the track to pass Busch and Montoya. Edwards had all the momentum coming out of turn 4. But just when it appeared that Edwards would blow by Bayne, the young driver made a veteran move. Bayne steered low onto the track to cut off Edwards and keep himself in the lead.

Instants later when the checkered flag waved, Bayne crossed the line first to win the Daytona 500 by .118 seconds!

Bayne had won by a blink of an eye. Well, actually it takes the human eye three times *longer* to complete a

REUTERS/Brian Blanco/Landov

Trevor crosses the finish line first as the checkered flag waves overhead.

blink than the time that separated Bayne and Edwards at Daytona ... so Bayne won by less than a blink of an eye!

"This is unbelievable," shouted the TV announcer. "This is fairy tale stuff."

Even Bayne had a hard time believing it.

"I keep thinking I'm dreaming," he said in Victory Lane. "Our first 500—are you kidding me? To win our first one in our second-ever Cup race, I mean, this is just incredible."

Gilliland took third in the race with Labonte and Busch right behind.

The stunned fans went wild cheering for Bayne when he spun out his tires on the track, creating a huge cloud of black smoke. Then he drove into the grass infield to turn a couple donuts.

Almost immediately, Bayne's car was surrounded by his Wood Brothers Racing pit crew. They pulled him out of the car and carried him around on their shoulders. It had been thirty-five years since this fabled racing team had won at Daytona.

Bayne jumped back in the car and rolled back onto the track, and that's where he made his first mistake of the day—he missed the turn to Victory Lane and had to backup.

"I didn't know how to get to Victory Lane," Bayne admitted to reporters with a boyish laugh.

And among the first people to greet him in Victory Lane were his parents, Rocky and Stephanie. The pair had watched the race from the grandstands instead of pit row because Rocky tends to get a bit loud in cheering

John Raoux/AP Images

Trevor celebrates in victory lane after winning the Daytona 500 NASCAR auto race at Daytona International Speedway in Daytona Beach, Florida, Sunday, Feb. 20, 2011.

for his son. But as soon as the race was finished, Rocky and Stephanie rushed to the track where a security guard stopped them. After Rocky showed his identification, the security guard not only let them onto the track but also gave Rocky the checkered flag to take down to his son.

Instantly reporters, fans, and even competitors were drawn to Trevor's genuine excitement, humbleness, and character.

"Second place in the Daytona 500 feels way worse than any other position I've ever finished in the Daytona 500," Edwards said after the race. "But that is made better by listening to Trevor and how excited he is. He is really a nice young man, a great guy to represent this sport with this win."

Bayne doesn't just want to represent NASCAR well; he has higher goals in mind. Since praying to accept Jesus Christ as his Savior as a teenager, Bayne has strived to stay focused on his faith in all he does.

Even before slipping into his fireproof driver's suit and donning his helmet at the start of the Daytona, Bayne had given over the results to God. He attended a chapel service early in the morning inside the Daytona garage and prayed with his team on pit road.

"We prayed right before the race started," Bayne said. "I just wanted everybody to be a part of it. I want to model myself after Jesus and follow in His footsteps. It was so cool to have a team that supported that."

Bayne credited God with allowing him to maintain balance and focus during the Daytona 500 and helping him keep a level head during those heart-pounding last laps.

But there was no way Bayne could prepare himself for the media blitz and fame that was about to come.

Flag Formula

For more than five hundred years, flags have been used to communicate during war. And for over sixty years, flags have been important communication tools to drivers as they do battle on NASCAR racetracks.

Eight main flags are used in NASCAR races:

- A **green** flag signals the start of a race. It's also used to let the drivers know the track is clear following a caution flag, and they can start driving fast and passing each other again.

- Drivers better slow down when they see a **yellow** caution flag. This flag signals that there's an accident or debris on the track, or that the track is no longer raceable due to bad weather. During a caution flag, the drivers can't pass each other and often bunch up behind a pace car. (Racetracks provide a pace car to keep the speeds under control at the beginning of a race and during cautions.)

- A **red** flag demands immediate attention. It means the track is unsafe and drivers must exit the raceway and stop. A red flag is waved when an accident blocks the track or if a driver is injured and needs quick medical attention. Heavy rains may also bring out a red flag.

- The **white** flag is used once during a race — it means one lap to go!

- Drivers don't like to see the **black** flag. Normally, this flag is waved at one particular car because it has broken a rule or has a mechanical problem. When a driver gets a black flag, he must make an immediate pit stop.

- If a driver doesn't stop right away after seeing a black flag, he is shown a **black with white cross** flag. This means he's been disqualified and won't score any NASCAR points for the race until he comes into the pits.

- The **blue with yellow stripe** flag is also called the "courtesy" flag. If a driver sees this flag, it's saying, "Move over. There are faster cars coming from behind." The slower car does not have to move over, but after receiving the courtesy flag, it's the nice thing to do.

- NASCAR drivers love being the first one to cross the line when a **black-and-white checkered** flag is waving. It signals the race is over. The first one to cross the line during a checked flag is the winner.

Chapter 2

Daytona Speed-Away

As soon as Trevor Bayne's number 21 Ford took the checkered flag at the Daytona 500, the TV announcer spoke the truest words he'd said all day: "That is a life-changing experience right there, buddy. Even at twenty years old."

Maybe he should've said, *Especially* at twenty years old." Normally when a driver wins at Daytona he's had years of experience dealing with the media and people vying for his attention.

NASCAR legend Dale Earnhardt had competed in "America's Race" twenty times before he won his first Daytona 500 in 1998.

At twenty years and one day old, Bayne became the youngest and least experienced driver to ever win this fabled race (see "Racing at Daytona"). Jeff Gordon had been the youngest Daytona winner when he won in 1997 at twenty-five years, six months, and twelve days old. And before Bayne's heroics on February 20, 2011, the only driver to win in his first attempt at the Daytona 500 was NASCAR pioneer Lee Petty—who won the very first race in 1959 (after all, somebody had to be the first winner).

But from the moment Bayne pulled into Victory Lane, it was obvious that this young man was mature beyond his years.

"I think the world is going to like him a lot," Carl Edwards said. Edwards knew Bayne from competing against him the previous year in the Nationwide series.

Edwards was right. Of course, there's a lot to like when it comes to Bayne, especially his boyish excitement, Southern charm, and all-American good looks. At a post-race press conference, Bayne had reporters laughing as he recounted the race—a race he still couldn't believe that he had won. "Sorry if I'm bouncing around on questions and answers," he said. "I figure I can do whatever I want, since this is just a dream anyway."

Heading into Daytona, Bayne felt fortunate just to be in the forty-three car field. While the favored drivers often bring an extra suitcase just in case they win and have to jet all over the country doing interviews, Bayne showed up in Florida in his F-150 pickup with just a couple of T-shirts. "I guess I better call somebody who can make up a suit and get some clothes down here for me," Bayne joked.

But when he was asked what he was thinking about when heading into the last lap, Bayne got serious. "In my opinion, I didn't know we were going to win," he said. "I thought it was cool just to say we led on the last lap of the 500."

It's even cooler to say he won.

Many Daytona 500 winners have been known to celebrate into the wee hours of the morning. Not Trevor Bayne. He had dinner with his race team at a hamburger place, then goofed around with his friends in the Speedway's infield RV lot.

"I went to dinner, then I did go to the basketball court for a game of horse ... and I lost," he said. "We were just shooting around, and then we rode our skateboards for a minute and tried not to break any legs. I went to bed shortly after that because I knew [the next day] would be a long one."

That *night* was a long one for Rocky. Bayne's father realized that his son's laundry needed to be done, so he found himself in a laundry room at three a.m.

But when Trevor woke up in the morning, his clothes were clean, packed, and he was ready to go. After breakfast with racing media in Daytona Beach, Florida, Bayne boarded a plane to fly to ESPN headquarters in Bristol, Connecticut. He appeared on "SportsCenter" and then flew to Chicago for four additional appearances. He made a stop at the "Ellen DeGeneres Show," along with other interviews in California. Trevor even got phone calls from Denver Broncos quarterback Tim Tebow and vice president Joe Biden.

Bayne took time out on Tuesday for NASCAR's teleconference that brought in a couple of media outlets that

Gary W. Green/Orlando Sentinel/MCT via Getty Images

Trevor had to immediately get used to cameras and media everywhere he went. Here he leaves his foot imprints in cement in Victory Lane after winning the Daytona 500.

normally don't call in to ask questions: *Christianity Today* and *Sports Spectrum*. While other reporters asked about the race and its aftermath, the newcomers wanted to know more about Trevor's faith—and he welcomed the questions. "The goal is not to be the best racecar driver," Bayne said. "It's not to be the most marketable; it's not to be the most popular. It's about building a platform and letting God use us on the platform He's building."

Bayne's name was suddenly everywhere. He had to check into hotel rooms under an assumed name. Heading into Daytona, Bayne could walk around the track without garnering much attention. Now he was stopped by fans everywhere he went.

"Let's just say it's like walking around with an older Justin Bieber," Corey Wynn, Bayne's publicist, said to Marty Smith of ESPN.com. "Trevor has fans of all ages. But in the twelve-to-eighteen female category, it is very high. I thought we were going to get mobbed during the media stop in San Francisco. The response has been surreal."

Trevor felt blessed to be in the position that God had put him in, but in the months to come, Bayne would have to deal with an unexpected and frightening health issue. One day, he could see fine—the next morning he woke up and his world was a blur.

One thing that never got blurry was his faith in Christ and desire to stay humble in all circumstances.

"I definitely think humility is something to hang onto for everybody," Bayne said. "All the young kids who are doing their sports, just stay grounded. Remember that if it wasn't for somebody else helping you, you wouldn't be sitting where you are. I've had so many people help me along the way that kept me grounded."

Nobody kept him more grounded than his parents.

Racing at Daytona

Daytona Beach, Florida, is known for two things: a beautiful, long stretch of sand and auto racing.

Daytona International Speedway is the largest outdoor stadium in Florida. With more than 168,000 permanent seats, this venue has witnessed some of the most memorable moments in stock car racing.

The Daytona 500 is the biggest, richest, and most prestigious race in America. But without the efforts of one man, this 480-acre motorsports complex might never have come into existence.

Starting in 1938, William H.G. France, also known as "Big Bill," promoted beach racing in Daytona. Ten years later, France was instrumental in creating the National Association for Stock Car Auto Racing, better known as NASCAR. His Daytona Beach and Road Course stretched 4.2 miles and was a tremendous success.

But France knew the days of beach racing were running out. Houses and hotels were being built up and down the coastline. In the mid–1950s, France started planning to build a speedway in the Daytona Beach area. He found a 480-acre plot of land near Daytona's airport and signed a fifty-year lease with the Daytona Beach Racing and Recreation District. France worked with Daytona Beach civil engineer Charlie Moneypenny on the design of the track. Since the land was squeezed between the airport and a road (now called International Speedway Boulevard), Moneypenny and France created a unique design: a racetrack that looked like a triangle with rounded edges. The men called it a "tri-oval," a description that is used to this day.

It took more than a year to construct the course, which measures 2.5 miles and features sweeping turns on either end of the track. Those turns stand almost four stories high and are banked at thirty-one degrees. The idea was to create a track where the driver could go full speed around the entire course. On most racetracks, a driver must brake, downshift, or let off the gas pedal to negotiate a turn.

France did not have a lot of money, but he was well connected with the business community and had a can-do attitude. Construction continued right up to the raceway's opening in 1959. When competitors saw the track for the first time, their reactions ranged from awe to outright nervousness. Daytona International Speedway was twice the size of any track these stock car drivers had ever raced on.

The inaugural Daytona 500 — actually called the "500 Mile International Sweepstakes" — was held on February 22, 1959. The event featured cars that looked much like the automobiles for sale at dealerships. But the racing was exciting as three cars crossed the finish line at approximately the same time. Johnny Beauchamp was declared the winner and went to Victory Lane. Lee Petty, who was scored second, protested the finish. Three days after reviewing film and photographs, France declared Petty the winner. Petty's margin of victory — just two feet — is still the closest winning margin in race history.

Richard Petty, Lee's son, holds the record for the most Daytona 500 victories at seven. He won the first time in 1964 and claimed his final victory in 1981.

Chapter 3

It Started in Knoxville

When Stephanie Bayne looks at her son, Trevor, she still sees the little baby she and her husband, Rocky, brought home from the hospital in late February 1991.

Sure, he's grown up. But some things haven't changed. Through the years, Trevor has consistently acted more mature than his age and proven to be a fast learner.

One moment in time remains stuck in the proud mother's mind. She and Trevor were sitting in a booth at a restaurant. The toddler was still in diapers and just starting to form words. Something caught his eye in the window, and he turned to his mom and said, "Mom, is that a reflection in the window?"

"I was like, 'Wow! Where did that come from?'" Stephanie recalls. "People say to me all the time that Trevor seems beyond his years."

Trevor has also performed beyond his years when

The Bayne family

Trevor (age 2) practices his driving skills very early on in his battery-powered toy car.

sitting behind a steering wheel. The Baynes bought a slow-moving, battery-powered toy car for Trevor when he could barely walk.

The toddler quickly wore out the car, driving it anywhere it could go. Soon Rocky found a tiny-tot dirt bike, which was made to take a pounding. Rocky put training wheels on the bike to make sure Trevor wouldn't fall. The training wheels came off when Trevor was four, but Rocky soon realized he'd made a mistake.

"One day in the backyard, Trevor went screaming by us," Rocky remembers. "Right then I told myself, *I have got to get that boy something that has four wheels on it, or he will kill himself on that bike.*"

The Bayne family

Trevor on his dirt bike.

So when Trevor turned five, his father bought him a used racing go-kart.

"I thought it would be a way to spend more time with him," Rocky said. "It was safer than the dirt motorcycle."

When the go-kart arrived, Trevor didn't react the way his father had hoped. Instead of being excited, the preschooler looked upset. Sure, the go-cart sported a number 24, the same as Trevor's favorite NASCAR driver Jeff Gordon (see "What Is NASCAR?"), but it wasn't the same color as on Gordon's "Rainbow Warrior" DuPont stock car.

"I was upset because the numbers on the go-kart were orange instead of yellow," Trevor says. "At the time, I didn't realize you can change the numbers. I told my parents, 'I want to be like Jeff.'"

Soon Trevor started following in Gordon's footsteps. Gordon began racing quarter midget cars when he was five. Trevor also began racing at local dirt tracks at a young age and quickly dominated his age class. There was no question that Trevor had natural talent behind the wheel.

Looking back, the arrival of the go-kart ultimately changed the lives of the Bayne family forever. "It's wild to think that's where all this started," Trevor says. "I could have been like any other kid, but it was just that one moment that had to happen."

Trevor in his new go-kart.

Well, that moment and a lot of help and support from his parents. Bayne would be the first to say it takes more than God-given ability to become incredibly good at doing something, whether it is playing piano, kicking a soccer ball, or driving a racecar. Trevor knows the link between turning his potential into success was his parents. Growing up, he had a nice balance with Rocky and Stephanie. He tried other sports in his youth, including baseball and football, but Trevor always came back to racing, because that's what he enjoyed the most. "Nobody made me do it," Bayne says about racing. "It was cool to have parents who could financially support it and give up their time. My dad was great. We never went to easy tracks. We raced where it would be tough."

His dad was eager to see him succeed in racing. His mom was always concerned about his safety. Trevor had wondered why his mother always worried about his racing, until one day when Trevor was watching his little brother Trey (thirteen years younger) zoom around a high school parking lot in a go-cart.

"That was the first time in my life that I noticed all the telephone poles and curbs," Trevor says. "Racing is a little more scary if you're not the one driving the go-kart or racecar."

Watching her son drive at break-neck speeds wasn't Stephanie's only sacrifice. She also missed spending weekends and holidays as a family. Often she'd be at home with Sarah (Trevor's little sister, who's four years younger) when Rocky and Trevor went out on the racing circuit.

The Bayne family

Trevor during one of his many go-kart races.

Rocky remembers driving to Daytona Beach on Christmas Day so Trevor could compete in a prestigious World Karting Association (WKA) national championship. Rocky and Trevor were always on the move.

"We would be gone three days a week, racing three classes a day," Rocky says of those continual go-kart seasons. "We raced forty-three weekends out of the year."

With Trevor gaining experience and racing on tough tracks, Rocky gradually realized his son needed to move up an age division in order to learn more about the sport.

"When he was eight, he'd run against ten- and eleven-year-olds," Rocky said. "When he was ten, he'd run against teenagers. When he was twelve, he'd run against adults. It was always about development, trying to make him a better driver. When he started beating the older kids, we'd move up."

This wasn't a father trying to live out a sports fantasy through his child. Trevor wanted to race from the day he hopped into the seat of that go-kart. He enjoyed the challenge of racing older, more experienced drivers, and he liked spending time with his father.

"Just when Trevor was about to win the championship, Rocky would move him up into a tougher class," Stephanie remembers. "Rocky always just pushed him to the next level. Trevor always had the confidence he could do it."

But it's not like Bayne never won a championship. Between the ages of five and thirteen, Trevor won three WKA world championships, three WKA Grand National Championships, nine Tennessee state championships, five Florida state championships, and two South Carolina state championships.

During NASCAR media day at Daytona International Speedway, February 10, 2011, Trevor talked about his history of competing against older drivers. "When you set your expectations and you finally get there, it doesn't come as a surprise," he said when asked why he didn't appear jittery on NASCAR's biggest stage. "Since I was five years old I wanted to be here. So now that we're here, we're gonna try to make a statement that we're not just here to run a race—we're here to stay."

Obviously, Trevor still had a way with words.

Stephanie knows that God has had a hand on her son, keeping him safe in all the races and dangerous situations. A verse has stuck with her since the time Trevor was young.

"It's Jeremiah 29:11," she says softly. " 'For I know the plans I have for you,' declares the Lord, 'plans to prosper you and not to harm you, plans to give you hope and a future.'"

And the Lord had a plan to make Trevor a great race-car driver.

What is NASCAR?

NASCAR is an acronym that stands for the National Association for Stock Car Auto Racing. Founded in December 1947 by William H.G. France and Bill Tuthill, it brought together a collection of stock car tracks and promoters that had no real organization. To imagine what that was like, picture the National Football League without a central office to schedule games, make rules, and negotiate television contracts.

In 1948, France called dozens of key drivers, car owners, and track promoters to Daytona Beach, Florida, to write a standard set of rules and create a series of races. These races not only rewarded competitors with money, but national championship points as well. The driver who gathered the most points would be declared the champion.

At first, NASCAR was known as the sport of the South because the majority of racing events were held in the Southeast region of the United States. Today, NASCAR is the most popular spectator sport in the United States with races held everywhere from Massachusetts and Florida to Arizona and California.

NASCAR oversees three main series of races: the Sprint Cup Series, the Nationwide Series, and the Camping World Truck Series.

The top racing tour is called the Sprint Cup Series, which actually didn't start until midway through NASCAR's second year of existence. The first Sprint Cup Series race—known then as the Strictly Stock Series—was held on June 19, 1949, at the Charlotte (N.C.) Fairgrounds. The race was won by Jim Roper from Great Bend, Kansas. NASCAR's universal set of rules came into play in the inaugural race. A driver named Hubert Westmoreland won the 200-lap race by a margin of four laps. But his Ford failed NASCAR's post-race inspection, and Roper was declared the winner. Roper won $2,000 for his efforts. Before Sprint Cup, the better-known racing machines were exotic cars built from the ground up and raced at places such as Indianapolis Motor Speedway, which celebrated its 100th anniversary in 2011. NASCAR's first season featured modified cars, or streetcars modified into racecars. The idea was to attract fans to racing by using the same cars many people owned. Competitors would buy a Chevrolet, Ford, Dodge, or any American-made sedan, weld in a roll cage and other safety features, and go racing.

The idea was a success from the first race, which attracted a whopping 13,000 spectators. From those humble beginnings, NASCAR has blossomed into a national sport, with super-sized speed arenas that accommodate up to 200,000 fans on race days!

Chapter 4

Follow the Rainbow Warrior

Once Trevor experienced the thrill of racing in a used go-kart, there was no turning back. As a youngster, he was completely hooked on motorsports. The *Knoxville News-Sentinel* offered this snapshot of Bayne's early racing career: "Raised to race in Knoxville, home to Thunder Road, the legendary thoroughfare for the hard-driving (men) who gave birth to stock car racing ... young Trevor soon began racing, earning three world championships by the time he was thirteen."

But well before his teen years, Bayne became a huge NASCAR fan. And nobody was more popular or successful during Bayne's developmental years than Jeff Gordon. So, of course, Gordon was Bayne's favorite driver.

Bayne grew up wearing the colors of Gordon's "Rainbow Warriors," a nickname given to the number 24 Hendrick Motorsports team for their brightly colored stock

Young Trevor with his childhood idol, Jeff Gordon.

car and uniforms. His room was decorated with racing posters, and he carried a Jeff Gordon lunch box to school.

Rocky and Stephanie weren't extremely wealthy while Trevor was growing up. They lived in a suburb of Knoxville, Tennessee, and ran a floor care company called Master America Corp. Their company provided for the family and also gave them some interesting perks, such as attending Food City nights at Bristol Motor Speedway (a highlight for Trevor). Food City, a chain of grocery stores, was one of Rocky's biggest clients during the mid-1990s.

During one race at the Bristol Motor Speedway, Jeff Gordon's crew chief set up a once-in-a-lifetime photo-op for the impressionable child. Ray Evernham took the camera from Rocky and snapped the picture himself, one of young

The Legendary Jeff Gordon

Jeff Gordon was a new breed of stock car driver. Born in Southern California, when Gordon was thirteen, he moved to Indianapolis, home of the Indy 500, to pursue more racing opportunities. By the time Gordon was nineteen, he raced full-time in the Nationwide Series. At twenty-two, he'd notched his first two Winston Cup victories (now called Sprint Cup). Then in 1995, at the tender age of twenty-four, Gordon earned his first Winston Cup Series championship. In 1996, when Trevor Bayne was five-years-old, Gordon was the defending Cup champion en route to a ten-win season.

Trevor in his number 24 jacket, with Jeff Gordon's hands on Trevor's shoulders. "Jeff was his role model," Rocky said.

Trevor did not only follow Gordon's love for racing, Trevor also followed Gordon's love for Jesus Christ. In the 1990s, Gordon was one of the few drivers to praise God in post-race television interviews, which caught the attention of Bayne's parents.

"Years ago when you thought of a devout Christian in racing, I would say 'Jeff Gordon,' because he was never afraid to put his faith out there," Stephanie says. She could not think of another driver who was so open about his faith.

Trevor said his parents raised him Christian, and they attended church while he was growing up, but just like standing in a garage won't make a person a car mechanic, sitting in church doesn't make somebody a Christian.

"I grew up in Christian home, went to church all my life, but I didn't really know God personally. On September 13, 2005, when I was a freshman in high school, I went to a revival with one of my friends, and that was the first time God started working on my heart.

I knew of him, but I didn't know him personally, and what he was capable of. It was the first time I really experienced his power, and I was in tears, just crying, and wondering why I was crying." He returned home and shared with his mother.

"I just remember him coming in the door that night," Stephanie says. Stephanie knew that this was a pivotal moment in her son's life. "It really hit home, the reality of God's presence in his life," she said.

"My mom and I started praying by the side of the couch, and I'll never forget that," Trevor said. "I felt the Holy Spirit come into me and work on me, filling my heart. I really wanted God to start running my life. I had to be willing to give it up, willing to give it all to God. And I did. I said, 'My life is yours.'"

From then on, Trevor let God do the steering. It was such a big moment in his life that Trevor remembers the exact day it happened—September 13, 2005.

And God led Trevor down one race track after another. It took time, money, and personal sacrifices, but he and his family knew that Trevor had been given special talents. They trusted in God, and Rocky and Trevor logged thousands of miles a year looking for stiffer racing competitions throughout the South and beyond. And Trevor continued to win at every level.

In 2005, Bayne won the Allison Legacy Series national championship. Considering he was racing against drivers twice his age, Trevor's statistics were unheard of—twenty-two starts, twelve victories, fourteen pole positions, and nineteen top-five finishes.

Trevor with his crew after winning the Allison Legacy Series, 2005.

With a championship in hand, Bayne had nothing more to prove in the Allison Legacy Series. It was again time to move on.

NASCAR 101
Specifics of a Sprint Cup Race Car

When NASCAR started, cars were bought off the showroom floors of dealerships, upgraded with safety equipment, and raced. Each race team built its own stock car from the bottom up. Those days are long over. The cars raced today are computer designed specifically for racing. You won't find a stereo system, GPS, or air conditioning. They weigh 3,400 pounds, travel over 200 miles per hour, and have eight-cylinder engines that produce around 800 horsepower — roughly ten times greater than a normal street sedan. Temperatures in the car can reach more than 120 degrees. Drivers wear five-layer fireproof suits, so they may lose as much as ten pounds during the race — in sweat! NASCAR drivers also have to deal with incredible forces in the car. When they take a turn at 160 mph, the G-forces pushing against their bodies make them feel like they're two or three times heavier. So a 150-pound driver may experience 450 pounds of force against him during a corner at Daytona.

The Sprint Cup Series Champion

NASCAR determines the champion each year based on collected championship points for each race. A driver earns forty-three points for winning a race. Second place is worth forty-two points and so on. The driver who finishes last gets one point. One bonus point is awarded per race if a driver leads for one lap or more. A bonus point can also be earned by leading the most laps in a race. The last ten races of the season, called the "Chase for the Sprint Cup," are limited to drivers who are tenth or higher in points. Drivers who have picked up a victory and are eleventh to twentieth in points also qualify. Starting in 2011, NASCAR allowed drivers to compete for only one NASCAR championship of its three national series — Sprint Cup, Nationwide, and Camping World Truck. Trevor Bayne received no points for his Daytona 500 victory, because he had already declared that he was competing for Nationwide Series points. After the last ten races, the driver who gathers the most points wins the Sprint Cup championship.

The NASCAR Racing Season

The NASCAR Sprint Cup Series has the longest season in professional sports. It starts in February with Speedweeks at Daytona International Speedway and ends in November at Homestead-Miami Speedway. There are thirty-six races that award championship points and five additional races that do not carry points. The Sprint Cup Series competes on mostly oval-shaped courses. The schedule takes competitors all over the country, from New York to California. Most teams take time off during December then start preparing for the season in January.

The Cost of Racing

For one car, one driver, and one crew, it costs around $20 million a season to own a race team. Most teams have sponsors, or companies that pay to label the cars and uniforms with their name and logos. Car owners have lowered their overall cost by fielding more than one car. In 2011, car owners Jack Roush, Rick Hendrick, and Richard Childress all had four cars they ran every weekend. Others have two or three cars. Seven-time champion Richard Petty is credited with the idea of having a full time sponsor for his race team. In 1972, he signed up with STP, which makes automobile lubricants, and had the STP logos on his racecars. He was paid $100,000 by STP that season. Many teams today have multiple sponsors, plus get millions of dollars in prize money each year.

Chapter 5

Up the Ladder

For Trevor Bayne to move up the racing ladder, he literally had to move. At the ripe old age of fifteen, he moved out on his own to Mooresville, North Carolina, and drove for his dad's racing team in the USAR Pro Cup Series. Behind the wheel of the number 29 Ford Late Model, Bayne became the youngest driver to win Rookie of the Year honors.

On the racetrack, Bayne made everything look easy. But things weren't always as easy away from racing. Because Trevor was immersed in motorsports from a young age, he missed having a normal childhood. Trevor didn't do many, common "kid" things. He was always racing.

"He had to grow up a little faster than most children," Stephanie says. "He missed the dances and birthday parties and things like that."

Trevor agrees he missed parts of a typical childhood. "At the time, it may have seemed like the end of the world when I couldn't hang out with friends," he says. "Racing takes *a lot* of sacrifice, but that's why only a few get to do this every weekend."

Part of that sacrifice meant moving to Charlotte. Rocky and Stephanie found Trevor a safe place to live, helped move his belongings, and then he was basically living on his own and finishing high school on the Internet. And even though he was racing cars, he didn't have a legal driver's license. "My crew chief would actually come pick me up, take me to the shop, and then drop me off at night."

Rocky visited Charlotte as often as possible. When Trevor first made the transition, Rocky would leave his wife and two younger children (Trevor's younger siblings Trey and Sarah) and stay in Charlotte for a couple days every week. "For my family to be supportive, it helped me get through," Trevor says. "I think the move was the best thing that I did for my career."

Just before Bayne turned sixteen years old, Dale Earnhardt Inc. (DEI) offered him a driver development contract. The contract required daily attendance at the famed DEI "Garage Mahal," a gigantic race shop located immediately north of Charlotte.

Despite his impressive racing resume, Trevor did not land a large signing bonus for his DEI contract. In other sports, such as baseball, talented players in their teens are often given millions of dollars in bonuses just for signing up. Not so with this Trevor. It was lean, but it enabled him to get both feet in the door of a high-profile NASCAR Sprint Cup Series operation. "Being in the shop, getting to know the guys, I showed them that I wanted to be here — that I wasn't a driver who just showed up on the weekends."

Trevor worked fulltime in the DEI shop and raced under the Dale Earnhardt Inc. banner in NASCAR K&N East Pro Series competition. Bayne loved being behind the wheel, but while at DEI he also developed some strong skills as a mechanic. He spent eighty percent of his time in the shop.

"When he worked at DEI, he was paid by the hour," Rocky says. "That was his pay for driving in the development program. He helped at the shop and worked on his own racecars. If he wrecked it, he had to cut the body off it. But he loved doing it."

His first start came in 2007 at the Mansfield Motorsports Speedway in Ohio. Trevor was just sixteen when he revved up his engine on the half-mile, paved oval of his first NASCAR race.

But unlike his debut in the Daytona 500, this race proved to be forgettable. He ran twenty-two laps before his engine quit running in lap twenty-three of the 150-lap race.

Despite a poor beginning, Bayne took full advantage of his chance to show his skills behind the wheel. In a three-race span, Bayne finished third at Watkins Glen International, a tricky road course in New York State. He came in second at New Hampshire Motor Speedway, a flat, one-mile oval. He made all thirteen starts in the

2008 K&N East Series, posting eight top-ten finishes and placing in the top-five, six times. The highlight of the season came when Bayne claimed the pole position at the Thompson Speedway in Connecticut for the Pepsi Full Fender Frenzy 100.

The Thompson race track is a .625-mile oval that's famous for its modified cars with no fenders. Bayne helped make it even more famous by celebrating his first NASCAR victory on July 12, 2008. Starting from the front of the pack, Bayne led for thirteen laps. And he was at the front when it counted—on the last lap. The victory earned his team $8,815.

For the season, Bayne completed ninety-eight percent of the 1,752 laps of competition. He was in the lead for ninety-five laps and finished fourth overall in points.

Good Start

Getting off to a good start is important in any race. For NASCAR drivers, earning a good starting position begins well before each race day.

During the week leading up to a competition, teams take turns in qualifying races. Normally, drivers draw numbers to see who will try to qualify first. Most drivers believe picking a higher number is better, because usually a racetrack gets faster the more it's driven on.

NASCAR teams drive one at a time on the track in order of their number. Each car quickly gets up to speed before passing the starting line. Once the car passes the line, a stopwatch times how fast it makes a lap. The drivers get to make two laps around the track, and they get to use the time from their fastest lap. On race day, the driver with the fastest time starts in the front—the pole position.

Starting from the pole position boosts the chances of victory. Statistics show that the driver who earns the pole position wins about twenty-two percent of the time. Winning one out of every four races is pretty good odds!

The teen felt like he was on his way up through the DEI organization. Unfortunately, DEI was on the way down. The team literally shut down after the 2008 season. Team owner Teresa Earnhardt went into a partnership with car owner Chip Ganassi to form Earnhardt-Ganassi Racing.

The break-up of DEI was difficult for Trevor. He had worked hard. But at age seventeen, he was laid off and looking for the next door to open. "When Trevor was at DEI, they had more than four hundred employees and he knew them all," Rocky says. Bayne didn't land a job right away. But Trevor trusted God's leading, and just as God had brought people and opportunities to Bayne at just the right time in the past, God was about to do it again.

47

Chapter 6

A Little Help From His Friends

When Trevor Bayne relocated to Mooresville, North Carolina, in 2006, the fifteen-year-old not only became a favorite son in the race shops at Dale Earnhardt Inc., but he eventually found friendship and a second family in Brent Weaver and Michael McDowell.

Brent Weaver managed a NASCAR Nationwide Series team, and Michael McDowell was a driver for Michael Waltrip Racing. The common bonds between this trio were racing and faith. Bayne met Weaver first, following the 2008 race season, after he had lost his job at DEI. Bayne became friends with McDowell after signing a contract with Michael Waltrip Racing in 2009.

Even though Trevor and Brent are separated by fifteen years of age, they share the same spiritual path. Rocky, Trevor, and his younger brother, Trey, met Weaver for lunch in 2008 when Trevor was looking for a job.

"At the first lunch meeting we had, the first thing Trevor did was spill a glass of water in his lap," Weaver said. "We still laugh about that. We didn't have anything for him on our race team at the time, but he was at the top of our list of drivers to hire. We became friends." Weaver said he had found his "little brother" in Christ. When they got together again, Weaver shared more about his personal relationship with Christ.

Meeting Brent was a God thing. Trevor said he probably wasn't letting him have control at that time. "I'd started drifting away. I wasn't intentional about praying and reading, and I met this Brent Weaver, and I saw his faith and he helped me. That's when my fire got lit," Trevor said.

Through summer 2009, they continued to encourage each other. "It was cool to see Trevor get fired up about his faith and his relationship with Christ," Weaver said. "[Trevor's] walk with God is by far the most important thing to him. When we go camping or kayaking or hang out on the lake, we don't talk racing much. We talk about relationships." "Trevor is humble and has a pure heart, and God is working in his life," Weaver said.

Weaver loves the racing industry, but he's seen a lot of drivers follow after the wrong things. They chase sponsors. They chase a prestigious racing team. They chase a glamorous NASCAR lifestyle. At just twenty years old, Trevor has stayed humble and used his platform as a Daytona 500 champ to reach out to other people.

"Trevor is a humble, young kid who, with God's help, can change people's lives," Weaver said. "I just encourage him to stay on that track. He's had more temptations and his schedule has been out-of-control crazy. Along with the big platform, the enemy has more ways to get him further away from his walk. But Trevor's heart and desire is to serve the Lord."

In the weeks leading up to the 2011 Daytona 500, Trevor wanted to make sure his focus was on the platform given to him. During the 2010 season, he had been caught up in making appearances, and taking on responsibilities that pulled him away from sharing his faith and encouraging people. He sat down with Weaver and his management group and told his team that his renewed passion to be a light for Christ was more important to him than where he finished on the race track. This was the way it was going to be for Trevor from then on, and he wanted to be held accountable to this mission.

Two weeks later, Trevor won the Daytona 500. "He called me after the race and I'm sitting there watching the TV and I'm praying," Weaver said. "I wasn't crying, but I was completely speechless. We couldn't say anything to each other. We wanted to talk, but we were both speechless."

"The times I look back at him, it's not Trevor the driver for me—it's Trevor going out and creating relationships. My brotherhood with Trevor is the most important thing to me. Racing will come and go, but I know, when our time comes and we stand before Christ and are asked, 'What did you do with the time, talents, and treasures I gave you?' Trevor will do just fine."

What a testimony!

Michael McDowell and Trevor shared their testimonies with orphanage children on a mission trip with Back2Back Ministries in Mexico, November 2010.

Another close friend who deeply impacted Trevor's life is Michael McDowell. He and Trevor met when Trevor first started at Michael Waltrip Racing (MWR) in 2009. Michael had been with the team for a while, and he was able to introduce Trevor to people and show him the ins and outs of MWR. Michael, who still does driver coaching, road course development for MWR, and is a driver in the NASCAR Nationwide and Sprint Cup Series, noticed Trevor in chapel a few times. Their faith immediately drew them together.

"Words can be empty, especially in this [racing] industry, so you try to live out what you believe," McDowell says. Trevor's actions after his Daytona 500 win and the unexpected sickness are a testament to his faith. "He handled things differently than most twenty-year-old people would have," McDowell says.

Winning the Daytona 500 put Bayne on the map. But McDowell saw Bayne's ability well before he climbed behind the wheel on February 20, 2011.

"The first few races he ran in the MWR car [in 2009] were really strong. I always knew he had the ability and would go far in the sport. His career won't be defined by the Daytona 500. I think he'll win a lot more races."

McDowell has been impressed with how Bayne has handled the extra attention and media exposure because he hasn't changed. He's still true to himself and to God.

"Racing is what we love to do. At the same time, it doesn't define who we are, our character and how we treat people. Trevor isn't prideful. He looks at [winning the Daytona 500] like God gave him an incredible gift and opportunities, and this was all part of God's plan. Trevor is just thankful to be part of it," McDowell says. "That's completely different from most of the people in our sport. To be good in our sport, a lot of times you have to be extremely selfish. For a lot of [drivers], it's about them. It's about how they are going to beat the next guy and nothing else matters. To see a young, humble kid win the Daytona 500 was nothing short of miraculous."

Chapter 7

Looking for a Ride

A driver doesn't make it to the NASCAR Sprint Cup Series without working hard, proving himself in other racing series, and having a strong support group. It also helps to get a break or two.

In Trevor Bayne's case, he rose from the dirt ovals of go-kart racing to Daytona 500 champion in the span of eight years. He followed God's path and did most of the heavy lifting, but he would not have been racing a stock car in 2011 without the help of others. Bayne met two of the most influential people in his career at one of the lowest points in his career.

In 2009, DEI was no longer fielding a stock car, no longer doing driver development deals, and no longer employing four hundred people at its shop. Bayne had lost his job and was looking for the next opportunity.

"That was one of the few times he was down," Brent

54

Weaver says. "When DEI went away and he didn't have a ride, he was a seventeen-year-old kid in Charlotte with nothing."

With DEI out of the picture, Trevor and his father made the next opportunity happen themselves. Trevor had not driven a racecar for six months. As Rocky Bayne says, "Trevor needed to race."

Rocky contacted Jimmy Means, who agreed to lease them a racecar for a Nationwide Series race at Bristol Motor Speedway in Bristol, Tennessee. He called Bob Jenkins, an independent restaurant owner, for sponsorship money. Jenkins lived about thirty miles east of Knoxville.

In just two weeks, Rocky had put together a deal that got Trevor seat time in a Nationwide Series race, which is a step up from the K&N East Series.

"We brought the car over to the DEI shop and worked on it," Rocky remembers. "Guys who had lost their jobs at DEI came in to help as volunteers. DEI also gave us some stuff."

Trevor was excited to be competing on his "home track" in his Nationwide debut. He had great memories of watching races at Bristol with his dad. But on March 21, 2009, the Scotts Turf Builder 300 turned out to be a humbling experience. Trevor qualified twenty-sixth out of forty-three cars. His number 52 car was a couple of laps down when something broke. Trevor ended up finishing twenty-third.

"The car wasn't made to run that size track," Rocky says. "But Trevor did enough with what we had to open

Mike Bliss (1) spins out of control in turn four as Trevor Bayne (52) passes during the NASCAR Scotts Turf Builder 300 auto race in Bristol, Tennessee, Saturday, March 21, 2009.

some eyes. It was at that race where we met Danielle Randall-Bauer and Gary Bechtel."

Randall-Bauer owned a company called Everest Marketing Group. She became Trevor's business manager and introduced him to Bechtel, who had been in and out of racing as a car owner and sponsor. At the time, he was looking for a new opportunity with a young driver.

Mission accomplished. Trevor walked through the next doorway of his racing career.

"He's a great kid and wonderful role model," Randall-Bauer says of Bayne. "He's a people person and a very talented driver."

Bayne had an equally high opinion of Bechtel and Randall-Bauer. "Danielle Randall-Bauer introduced me to Gary Bechtel and his son," Bayne says. "They went with me to MWR (Michael Waltrip Racing) and formed that partnership. That's what gave me my spark into NASCAR."

Bayne had hoped to be a full-time driver with DEI. With that door closed, the eighteen-year-old jumped at the chance to sign with MWR.

After making his Nationwide Series debut at Bristol Motor Speedway in March with a team slapped together for the event, Bayne now had a contract with an established team and was scheduled to compete in eight Nationwide races.

"This was a tremendous opportunity, and I have to thank Gary Bechtel for taking a chance on me," Bayne said. After only a few months, Bechtel decided to invest in Bayne's talent. And it paid off. They'd found themselves an awesome driver.

Chapter 8

Nationwide on His Side

Dozens of great drivers wait for their big chance in stock car racing. Trevor Bayne didn't like to wait for things to happen. He was going to *make* them happen. The Michael Waltrip Racing team was founded by two-time Daytona 500 champion Michael Waltrip and funded by co-owner Rob Kauffman, an international financier with a passion for racing. In 2009, as part of the MWR team, Bayne made his second Nationwide start in a stock car prepared in the MWR race shop.

His first competition in premium race equipment came at Nashville Speedway on June 6, 2009. Bayne qualified the number 99 Aarons Toyota second on the grid at the Federated Auto Parts 300. Bayne was enthusiastic about the race.

Unfortunately, Bayne did not finish. Despite starting from the outside pole position (another name for the second spot), Bayne got swept into a five-car accident in turn four on lap 124. "We had a great car, but we just got caught up in somebody else's mistake," Bayne said afterwards. But he learned a lot that weekend, especially from crew chief Jerry Baxter.

Eight promised races quickly turned into twelve. Along the way, Bayne picked up two more races with car owner Bryan Mullet. Bayne's best race came on July 26, 2009, when he earned the pole position and led for thirty-four laps in the Kroger 200 at Indianapolis Raceway Park. His seventh place finish was his highest of the year.

Trevor Bayne (99) skids across the track after colliding with Carl Edwards (not shown) during lap two of the NASCAR Nationwide Series Carfax 250 auto race at Michigan International Speedway in Brooklyn, Michigan, Saturday, August 15, 2009.

His last appearance of the Nationwide season occurred in Phoenix, where he finished fourteenth after starting in thirty-seventh place. "We got to pass a lot of cars, that's for sure," he said after the race.

Bayne had hoped to finish higher. After moving up twenty-five places, he couldn't seem to catch up to the leaders. His pit crew made some adjustments to the car at every stop. But in the end, it wasn't quite enough. A driver can only drive; his car also has to perform.

Bayne ended the year in Central Florida. He wasn't racing at Daytona International Speedway, but testing at New Smyrna Speedway, a half-mile oval in Samsula, Florida—less than fifteen miles from NASCAR's premier racing facility.

New Smyrna Speedway is not affiliated with NASCAR, but many race teams use the track to collect data for competitions in places such as Phoenix, New Hampshire, and Martinsville Speedway. Bayne was there with MWR crew chief Bootie Barker and two former Formula One series drivers.

"Those guys are going to get most of the laps," Bayne told a handful of local media. "I'm here to help make sure the car feels the right way."

Bayne only had a half-season of Nationwide Series races under his belt, but MWR felt comfortable in sending the youngster to Florida to help test with a pair of veteran Formula One drivers.

For the season, Bayne drove fifteen Nationwide races—including the Bristol race—and scored seven top-fifteen and two top-ten finishes.

Kyle Busch won the 2009 Nationwide Series title, but Bayne had learned a lot and felt like he'd had a successful season.

"Considering I didn't even have a ride at the beginning of the 2009 season, I would have to say [it was a success]," Bayne said. "I really wish I could have grabbed a top five or even a win, but I learned a lot this season. In this series you have to have a little patience and realize there is plenty of time to make your way to the front. I think the track time that I received this year will definitely translate into top five finishes next season."

Bayne may not be a prophet, but his words rang true.

Young, Successful Drivers

Trevor Bayne is not the first young driver to enjoy wild success in the NASCAR Sprint Cup Series. Check out other drivers who tasted success early in their careers:

Kyle Busch

Busch started his career with car owner Rick Hendrick at Hendrick Motorsports in 2005. Busch became the youngest driver in NASCAR history to win during his rookie season. He was twenty years and 126 days old when he won the Sprint Cup race at California Speedway in 2005. Busch did not hold the record for youngest winning driver in series history for very long. Joey Logano claimed that mark in 2009.

Before Busch's victory, the previous record had been set by Donald Thomas, who won his first race at the age of twenty on November 16, 1952. Busch bested Thomas's age by four days. Heading into the 2011 Sprint Series season, Busch posted nineteen career victories. He now drives the number 18 Joe Gibbs Racing Toyota.

Jeff Gordon

Gordon made his NASCAR Sprint Cup Series debut in the last race of the 1992 season. It was a pass-the-torch moment in NASCAR. Gordon, who rolled to win four Sprint Cup championships (so far), was just beginning his career, while Richard Petty, a seven-time NASCAR champion, was competing in his last race.

Gordon earned Sprint Cup Rookie of the Year in 1993 at age twenty-two and won his first race in 1994. His first Cup Series championship came at the tender age of twenty-three. Three of Gordon's four championship runs happened before he turned thirty years old. In his early years, the media called him "Wonder Boy."

Going into the 2011 season, Gordon had eighty-two career Sprint Cup victories and $116 million in prize money. Since he first entered the Sprint Cup Series, Gordon has driven the number 24 Chevrolet owned by Rick Hendrick. Now with a bit of gray in his temples, Gordon turned 40 in August 2011.

Joey Logano

When Tony Stewart decided to leave Joe Gibbs Racing in 2009 to start his own Sprint Cup Series race team, the two-time NASCAR champion left big shoes to fill. Logano answered the call. Deemed "Sliced Bread" by the racing media, Logano started the 2009 Daytona 500 at the tender age of eighteen. About a month after turning nineteen that season, Logano won a Sprint Cup Series race at New Hampshire Motor Speedway, driving the number 20 Toyota.

Chapter 9

Trading Teams

The 2010 NASCAR Nationwide Series brimmed with brightness for nineteen-year-old Trevor Bayne. He had broken through and been recognized as one of the sport's up-and-coming stars. No more working on the stock cars he drove.

Bayne had committed to run a full season in the number 99 Diamond–Waltrip Racing Toyota, which included his first taste of racing at the Daytona International Speedway.

Because Gary Bechtel was involved in the team ownership, Bayne's official race team was called Diamond–Waltrip Racing. Bayne was classed as a "series regular," which meant if he finished well, he could contend for the overall Nationwide Series points title.

But with more opportunity, came more responsibility—such as chatting with the media at Daytona in January

2010 for its "Preseason Thunder" program. About two dozen drivers from NASCAR's three national series showed up to visit with race fans and talk about the Speedweeks program.

Bayne fielded a number of questions, like which racetrack he was most looking forward to tackling. "Daytona is where it all pretty much started," Bayne said. "It's going to be pretty crazy jumping out there with the sharks, so I'm looking forward to being a part of that."

When asked about racing against the better-funded, more-experienced Sprint Cup drivers who also competed in the Nationwide Series, Bayne got excited. "I think it's a great opportunity to excel," he said. "We had a lot of Cup drivers coming in last year, but that also created opportunities to learn. Getting to follow a driver like Carl Edwards around these racetracks is pretty cool."

About a month later, Bayne was back at Daytona to drive the number 99 Diamond–Waltrip Racing Toyota in the DRIVE4COPD 300 that pitted rising stars from the Nationwide Series against the proven winners of the Sprint Cup.

NASCAR star Tony Stewart won the race by a fraction of a second over Carl Edwards. Bayne didn't fare nearly as well. He qualified a respectable seventeenth, but crashed on lap seven to place forty-first out of forty-three cars.

Ironically it was the tandem racing style of Daytona that got the best of Bayne on February 13, 2010. Early in the race, Bayne was being pushed from behind by veteran Mike Bliss, who was trying to get both cars toward

Trevor sits on his No. 99 car during qualifying for the Nationwide Dollar General 300 auto race at Chicagoland Speedway in Joliet, Illinois, Friday, July 9, 2010.

the front of the pack. However, when Bayne lost control, it took out both drivers.

"It [the push from Bliss] was with all the right intentions," Bayne said after the race. "I hate that it happened so early in the race."

For the first couple of months, Bayne had difficulty making his mark in the number 99 Toyota. But in June of 2010, he started a string of solid finishes. It began with an eleventh-place finish at Kentucky Motor Speedway. Then over the next fifteen races, Bayne put up amazing numbers. He notched ten top-ten finishes, five top-five, and even started from the pole position in three consecutive events. At Gateway International Raceway, Indianapolis Raceway Park, and Iowa Speedway, Bayne had the fastest time in qualifying. And he capitalized on those great starts by placing in the top five every time. Those are the kind of finishes that win championships, but it was not going to happen with Diamond–Waltrip Racing.

Because of the tight economy, DWR was unable to find enough sponsorship funding to guarantee Bayne a ride in 2011. In a somewhat odd turn of events, Bayne raced the number 99 DWR Toyota on September 25, 2010. Then the following weekend he was behind the wheel of the number 17 Roush Fenway Ford at Kansas Speedway.

Since 2007 when Roush Racing joined with the Fenway Sports Group (owners of the Boston Red Sox), Roush Fenway Racing had become one of the most successful teams in NASCAR. Before Bayne's first race in Kansas, team owner and former driver Jack Roush released a statement that said: "We are pleased to be able to sign a driver of both Trevor's caliber and character. Trevor has exhibited a distinctive ability to run fast, up front, and compete side by side with veteran drivers in a relatively short amount of time. We feel that he possesses all of the tools necessary to grow into a top-level driver."

The week following his debut with Roush Fenway, Bayne told the *Sporting News* that Diamond–Waltrip Racing had missed a September 15 deadline to extend his contract into the 2011 season. If Bayne stayed with DWR, he risked being able to only compete in a partial season.

When Roush Fenway offered Bayne a full Nationwide ride for 2011, Diamond–Waltrip Racing decided to make a clean break. "I showed up at the shop, and my seat wasn't in the car," Bayne said. "I was like, 'Uh, what's happening?'"

It was his first experience with the business side of NASCAR. Few things stay the same in stock car racing, including custom-made driver seats. But Bayne fit nicely in the seat at Roush Fenway.

On the year, Bayne ran all thirty-five races in the Nationwide Series and finished with 1,598 points to place seventh overall in the standings. Brad Keselowski won the title.

Although the transition between teams late in the year wasn't easy for Bayne, he credited his faith in Jesus and his Christian upbringing for seeing him through. His faith had helped him then, and he'd continue to lean on it in the future.

The Need for Speed

More than fifty years *before* drivers competed in the first Daytona 500, the Dayton area had been known as "The Birthplace of Speed." From 1903 to 1935, Daytona showcased straight-line speed runs down its wide, hard-packed sand beach.

The first reported race was a two-car battle on the sands in neighboring Ormond Beach in 1903. Horace Thomas drove the Olds Pirate, while Alexander Winton competed in the Bullet number 1. They lined up side-by-side on the beach. *Automobile News* offered this report: "It was a glorious chase to watch from the bathhouse steps. The Bullet caught the Pirate just before the finish was reached and beat it by 1.5 seconds." The top speed in that race was just over sixty-eight miles per hour.

Soon the long, flat beach attracted the top automobile builders, competitors, mechanics, and equipment. Within two years, drivers topped the 100-mph mark. In 1927, Sir Henry Segrave did the unthinkable when he recorded a speed in excess of 200 mph driving the British-made Sunbeam.

His record stood until 1935 when Sir Malcolm Campbell brought his famed Bluebird Speed Machine from England. On March 7, 1935, Campbell broke the 300-mph mark for the first time in history. In order to make it an official land speed record, Malcolm was required to turn around the Bluebird and make another run in the opposite direction.

The Bluebird packed 2,500 horsepower and had an airplane-like look to it, including a tail wing. On his return trip, Malcolm nearly lost control of the big, blue, metal beast because the sand shredded his tires.

His two-run average was still a remarkable 276 mph. Watching from the safety of a sand dune was a young mechanic named William H.G. France, who had just moved to Daytona Beach from Washington, D.C. It was France who would later continue Daytona Beach's racing tradition.

Chapter 10

Confidence and Faith

Confidence and faith go hand in hand for Trevor Bayne. He's confident without being cocky, which is a rare quality at the top of stock car racing. Bayne trusts his ability and allows God to be the guiding force in his life.

Even Bayne's competitors, including five-time NASCAR Sprint Cup Series champion Jimmie Johnson, have taken note of his style and grace.

"He's a great guy," Johnson said. "I've known him for a long time and am very proud of his progress on and off the track."

If anything, Bayne gets criticized for being "too perfect." It's a criticism that other young Christian athletes, including Denver Broncos quarterback Tim Tebow, have heard.

"For his sake, I hope he dodges all the vanilla criticism or whatever could be there from trying to be a good person," Johnson added. "He's being who he is, and he's certainly fast and stands on the gas."

Arguably, no driver has come up through the racing ranks faster and achieved the success Bayne has enjoyed. By being in the spotlight, Trevor has also been able to shine a light on his faith.

"I feel so blessed," Bayne said after winning the Daytona 500. "I can't describe how crazy it is that God surrounded me with these quality people, quality equipment, and made it come together that perfect in our first-ever attempt."

Those aren't just words for Bayne. He truly looks at the Bible as a roadmap through life and knows that God is ultimately in control of what happens to him. Even though Bayne is constantly on the road, he makes time to study God's Word and learn more about Jesus.

"He goes to chapel all the time and supports Motor Racing Outreach (MRO)," Rocky says. "That's what he does."

MRO is a traveling racing ministry. Each NASCAR series has a chaplain. Because most Sprint Cup Series events happen on Sundays, MRO holds church services and Bible studies at the track before every NASCAR race. Former MRO chaplain, Lonnie Clouse, described Bayne as a faithful attendee at the Nationwide Bible studies, usually sitting in the front row, and willing to get up and read Scripture, open in prayer, or help in whatever was needed.

When Chaplain Clouse joined Back2Back Ministries, Bayne traveled with Clouse to Mexico to help serve abandoned and neglected children find homes. According to Clouse, Trevor made quite an impression. The kids huddled around him, played soccer and asked how fast he drove. "Most of them had no clue who he was and what he did."

Away from the racetrack, Bayne continues to volunteer his time to help people or organizations that

Trevor gives a young boy a piggyback ride.

Kilby/www.visionphotos.com

Trevor enjoys laughing and playing with the children.

are close to his heart. Less than a week before the 2011 Daytona 500, Bayne attended a charity fishing event for The Darrell Gwynn Foundation that raised money to buy wheelchairs.

In fact, some of his one million dollars in Daytona 500 prize money went to charities. "There are a lot of foundations and ministries that need support," Bayne said in a post-race interview. "Back2Back ministries in Mexico is one. We will help them out as much as we can."

Bayne doesn't brag about his faith. He doesn't hit people over the head with the Bible. His faith is just part of who he is, so it oozes out in a unique Christian charisma. "People are drawn to him," says Michael McDowell. "Because of his character and personality—being completely humble and thankful for the opportunity—Trevor is accepted."

Bayne also brings a child-like exuberance to everything he does. At times, he acts like a kid, which makes him stand out in the NASCAR Sprint Cup Series garage area. When he's praying or racing, he's serious. When he's playing or hanging out with family and friends, it's like watching a kid at the carnival.

When Bayne goes home to Knoxville, he still stays in the bedroom where he grew up as a kid.

"Trevor may be an adult in the eyes of the law, but he's still a kid to [us]," Rocky said, adding that his son can even get a bit irresponsible. "He went through about twenty cell phones in [2010]. He's always breaking them or losing them, and his room can still get a little messy."

Bayne may be a Daytona 500 champion and one of NASCAR's fastest rising stars, but he's trying to keep it all in perspective.

"I'm a twenty-year-old kid," he says. "I don't want to be changed by any of this success. I think these guys on my race team will keep me down to Earth. I'm sure they'd pop my bubble, and I'd expect them to. I'm a normal kid who's been really, really blessed and fortunate. My faith is obviously a big part of this, and that's really the reason I'm here. I think that's the reason why all of this worked out."

High Speed Outreach

Motor Racing Outreach (MRO) was founded by Max Helton in 1988. Helton was working at a church in Glendora, California, when he met racing legend Darrell Waltrip and his wife, Stevie. Helton told the couple he felt called to organize a ministry in auto racing. Soon after, Helton was leading Bible studies with drivers and crew members, holding chapel service at racetracks, and providing personal counseling sessions. Fourteen years later, Helton formed World-Span Ministries to take God's Good News to racing series around the world.

Helton left MRO in the capable hands of Billy Mauldin and Stephen Keller. This tandem has become two of the most recognized figures in NASCAR garages week to week. Mauldin and Keller may not have the star power of Sprint Cup drivers Jeff Gordon or Jimmie Johnson, but NASCAR officials, drivers, crew chiefs, mechanics, and race fans know them well.

Through the 2011 NASCAR season, Mauldin served as president and CEO of Motor Racing Outreach while Keller was the traveling chaplain for NASCAR's two most high-profile racing series. Each weekend Mauldin and Keller helped bring the message of hope and God's forgiveness to those who must work on Sundays.

In addition to stock car racing, MRO organizes programs for other forms of motor sports, such as motorcycle and powerboat racing. And MRO doesn't just minister to the drivers. It reaches out to fans, officials, and the media. MRO desires to support all of these racing communities so the people may enjoy a more whole-some life together and, in turn, become role models for millions of motor sports fans around the world.

Chapter 11

Tryout at Texas

When Trevor Bayne left Diamond–Waltrip Racing toward the end of the 2010 NASCAR Nationwide Series season and signed a contract with Roush Fenway Racing (RFR), the timing couldn't have been more perfect.

Bayne was now part of an established and successful team. And unknown to the young driver, RFR was in talks with Wood Brothers Racing—one of NASCAR's oldest teams (see "All in the Family"). The family-owned team had been racing since the early 1950s. But the modern sport of stock car racing had become so technical in such a short period of time that a family-owned, single-car team was no longer viable at NASCAR's highest level.

Near the end of the 2010 season, Len and Eddie Wood reached out to Ford Motor Company and Sprint Cup Series car owner Jack Roush for help. The Wood family had raced only Ford equipment since they began and wanted to stay loyal.

Tired from swimming against the tide of change, the Woods made a deal to have access to the vast resources of Roush Fenway Racing.

"It was just getting to the point that you couldn't quite get where you needed to get," Eddie said. "No matter how much money you spent, no matter how much work you did, you couldn't get to the point that you were competitive every week."

The Woods talked with Roush and worked out a plan. Ford and Roush responded by rushing in with sponsorship funding and new technology. But another part of that plan was to bring Bayne on as the driver of the number 21 Wood Brothers Racing Ford in the Sprint Cup Series.

Bill Elliott, the 1989 Sprint Cup Series champion, had driven for Wood Brothers in eleven races. When Roush signed Bayne to a Nationwide contract, he asked Eddie and Len to give Bayne a tryout in the AAA Texas 500 at Texas Motor Speedway to see if he could compete with Sprint Cup drivers.

When asked about the audition, Bayne giggled a bit.

"I wanted to get approval, so we could run in the 2011 Daytona 500," Bayne said. "If I didn't run Texas, we didn't know if I would be able to run at Daytona."

Bayne qualified twenty-eighth in the forty-three car field. He worked his way up and finished seventeenth, a great run for a driver with limited experience and making his first Sprint Cup start. The $96,625 payday

Robert Laberge/Getty Images for NASCAR

Trevor Bayne drives the #21 Motorcraft/Quick Lane Ford during practice for the NASCAR Sprint Cup Series AAA Texas 500 at Texas Motor Speedway on November 5, 2010 in Fort Worth, Texas.

wasn't too bad either. Denny Hamlin started two spots behind Bayne, but ended up winning on November 7, 2010, to take home $453,575.

"We were really successful," Bayne said. "We had an awesome day together. These guys, they feel like family. We clicked."

It may not have looked impressive on the race report—seventeenth at Texas Motor Speedway—but it truly was a big moment in Bayne's racing career. The teenager proved he had the stamina and skills to compete with the best.

"That was incredible," Bayne added as he emerged from the number 21 Ford. "These things are so much fun. I wish I could do it every weekend. It was a blast to drive, and to be that fast for a first run is incredible. I want to thank everyone for giving me this opportunity. That was as good or better than we expected."

Just the day before the AAA Texas 500, Bayne was the new guy with Roush Fenway Racing running in the 200 lap O'Reilly Auto Parts Challenge. He finished twelfth in that race. The following day he made his audition run in the Sprint Cup Series for Wood Brothers Racing.

"It's something I didn't expect to happen this year," Bayne said. "Once one door closed, another one opened—and it was a little bit bigger door."

After the 2010 season had run its course, Bayne was added to the 2011 package. It was decided he'd compete for the NASCAR Nationwide Series championship, plus run a part-time Sprint Cup schedule for Eddie and Len Wood. Roush thought it was a good fit—a young, inexperienced driver with NASCAR's oldest racing team.

Bayne may be young, but he knew the history of Wood Brothers Racing and the drivers who had competed for this legendary team.

"It's a cool list," he said. "It's incredible to be a part of that group, it really is."

Little did Bayne know that in a few months his name would be added to an even cooler list—that of Daytona 500 champion.

All in the Family

What do trees and auto racing have in common? Well, without the first, Wood Brothers Racing may never have come to be.

More than sixty years ago, Glen and Leonard Wood from Stuart, Virginia, bought a 1940 Ford and brought it home to fix into a racecar. Their father, Jay Walter Wood, was less than impressed with the idea.

The first thing he said was, "Don't unload that mess here!"

There was nowhere else to take it, so they parked it under a beech tree. To pull out the engine, the brothers threw a chain over the lowest branch of the tree and yanked it out.

"Our racing really started under a beech tree," Eddie Wood, Glen's son, said.

Eddie is proud of his family's racing tradition. Wood Brothers Racing formed in 1952 and was the top independent racing team for years.

Glen, who was inducted into the NASCAR Hall of Fame, was the driver. The brothers competed part-time for six years. The effort became much more serious in 1960 when Speedy Thompson and Glen combined to score five victories.

For the next twenty-five years, the team was a force to be reckoned with, attracting the top drivers of the era. The one driver most often linked to Wood Brothers's success is David Pearson. From 1972–78, Pearson made only 143 starts but won forty-three times in the number 21. Their most famous victory came at the 1976 Daytona 500. As Pearson and seven-time NASCAR champion Richard Petty approached the checkered flag, their cars tangled. Both spun off the Daytona International Speedway racing surface. Pearson was able to keep his motor running and took the win at about thirty-five mph. Petty's car was stuck in the grass.

In the 1980s, ownership of the team transitioned to Glen's sons, Eddie and Len. Since the late 1980s, "the little team that could" became "the team that did not win very often." From 1984 until 2010, Wood Brothers Racing tallied just five wins, the last with Elliott Sadler in 2001.

Some of NASCAR's biggest stars—many of whom are in the Hall of Fame—have driven the number 21, including Pearson, A.J. Foyt, Junior Johnson, Cale Yarborough, Dan Gurney, Marvin Panch, and Neil Bonnett. And now Trevor Bayne can be added to that list.

Chapter 12

Prepping for 2011

NASCAR Sprint Cup Series racing functions quite differently than other major sports. In the National Football League, each team has an owner, who hires a general manager and coach to find and train the players on the roster. The team is a franchise of the league.

In NASCAR, the process is much more complicated. First, a team needs to be formed. Second, that team has to have sponsorship money to race. This isn't like making a billboard or painting a sign to hang in center field of a baseball stadium. Sponsors spend up to $20 million a year for the right to have their company name on a stock car.

If a race team does not have the money to race, it is under no obligation to compete—unlike teams in the other major league sports. Another big difference? The majority of companies in NASCAR have a completely separate advertising budget to help promote their sponsorships. In Trevor Bayne's case, he not only drives the number 21 Wood Brothers Ford, but he also acts as a spokesman for Motorcraft Quick Lane, a brand in the Ford family.

Sometimes it sounds funny how a driver refers to his car after a race, like when Jimmie Johnson may say, "This Lowe's Chevy Impala was running really good." But the fact is, without sponsors the drivers couldn't race, so they truly appreciate and want to help the companies that make their racing dreams a reality.

The package for Bayne started coming together late in the 2010 season. Roush Fenway Racing crew chief Donnie Wingo left to work with Wood Brothers. The job of the crew chief is to get the best performance out of the car while keeping the driver safe. A crew chief is sort of like a football coach, while the driver is the quarterback. A crew chief keeps an eye on the race, formulates a plan, and constantly talks with the driver. But it's up to the driver to make things happen and let the crew chief know how the car feels on the track. The relationship between crew chief and driver is key to a successful team.

When Wingo first saw Bayne, the veteran crew chief said the young driver had all the qualities that make a solid stock car driver. "From the time he got in the car at Texas to the end of that race, you could see he is just one of those guys that has this knack," Wingo said. "The part I liked about Trevor was he did a real good job of racing for us. The way he was able to pass cars and not just sit and ride behind was a good thing. That is something that you can't teach these young kids; they just have to learn it on their own."

While many around the racing world knew a deal was all but done, the official announcement that Bayne would run for Wood Brothers Racing was made on January 20, 2011. Eddie Wood was particularly pleased that his sixty-year-old team would have a bright, young driver behind the wheel of the number 21 Ford.

"He is very mature for his age," Wood said. "He is very aware of what it takes to be a racecar driver in the Sprint Cup Series. He is good with his feedback in the racecar and all-around is ready to go racing, in every single aspect."

Eddie was impressed with the communication that Bayne and Wingo had when they raced in Texas and tested tires at Daytona a month later.

"That is where it starts, making sure that the crew chief and engineers and the people who are controlling what is in the car mesh with the driver," Eddie added. "So far it really seems to be doing that."

Wood Brothers was a particularly good fit for Bayne. Unlike many of NASCAR Sprint Cup Series teams, which field three or four stock cars each week and are more corporate, Wood Brothers Racing remains a family-owned team guided by Christian beliefs.

Bayne had known for a while that he would be driving the number 21 Ford, but had to keep it secret until Wood Brothers Racing and Roush Fenway Racing felt it was time to announce the union of driver, team, and sponsor. Those kinds of announcements generate a lot

Trevor enjoying a pre-Daytona road trip. While Trevor is very mature for his age, he still knows how to act young and have a good time.

of publicity for the teams, so it was kept secret until January—just a month before Daytona Speedweeks.

Once the news got out, Bayne could freely talk about his opportunity.

"I am just glad to finally be able to show my excitement," Bayne told the media during January's Daytona testing. "I have had to keep it bottled up for a few weeks.... I couldn't ask for a better team to be with to start out."

Bayne liked that it was a one-car team, so everybody could focus on his car. Plus, he had a lot of respect for Wingo and Len, Glen, and Eddie Wood. Wingo has children who are as old as Bayne, and the Wood brothers have been running their team for as long as Bayne has been alive. But the age difference is easily overcome by their shared passion for racing.

"I think [Donnie] looks at me like I am one of his kids sometimes," Bayne added. "The relationships here are almost overwhelming, because it is so easy. Everybody is really personable, especially Len and Eddie. They are great owners, and I couldn't ask for a much better situation."

Bayne knew he'd have to rely on his experienced team to get the most out of his own racing abilities. Bayne had always competed against older drivers, but now he was a rookie going against the best NASCAR drivers in the world. Instead of fearing the unknown, Bayne had a plan for success.

"If we can run top-fifteen finishes in those first five races, then that would set us up to be decent on the points," Bayne said. "That is what we need to do to try accumulating more sponsorship to keep going. We want to do as well as we can in the first five to help us set up the rest of the season."

A top-fifteen finish was indeed a high goal for his first Daytona 500, but that wasn't God's plan for him. For years, Bayne had known the verse Ephesians 3:20 that says, "Now to him who is able to do immeasurably more than all we ask or imagine, according to his power that is at work within us." And in a month, God would do "immeasurably more" than Bayne would have imagined.

Faithful Friends

NASCAR drivers live on the edge. Pushing the limits of their high-powered machines, they literally take their lives into their hands each weekend. Top-speed turns in tightly packed groups could lead to a fiery crash at any moment. With the possibility of dying so close at hand, it's not surprising that many top NASCAR drivers put their trust in Jesus Christ to keep them safe. They know that God can protect them on this earth, and if anything happens to them, then the same Lord would protect their eternities in heaven.

Because of their deep faith, many NASCAR personalities are not afraid to discuss their relationship with Jesus Christ. Check out a few of these testimonials gathered by Motor Racing Outreach:

Darrell Waltrip: Three-time Sprint Cup Series champion, now a television commentator for FOX Sports

"I've been a Christian since 1983, but even then I was more interested in what Darrell Waltrip wanted than what God wanted. As I began to grow as a Christian, I realized that there were things in life more important than winning races. I began to see that serving God needed to be first. God showed me just how blessed I was in having such a strong Christian wife and how children are a true blessing as well. The most important thing to do is to pray and study the Bible. God can take your need and bless you as well as others around you if you put Him first."

Dale Jarrett: 1999 Sprint Cup champion, now a commentator with ESPN

"I grew up in a Christian home. My parents made sure that we were in church. But as I grew up, I got sidetracked and didn't live my life as I should. But things changed when I started driving for Joe Gibbs. He was and is a man who is very strong in the Lord, and his influence on me helped get my life back to where it should be. My wife and I dedicated our lives to the Lord, and we know that our children are growing up in a Christian home. There's a lot of different ways to live your life, but there's only one right way — and that's to live for the Lord."

Jeff Gordon: Four-time Sprint Cup Series champion

"I welcomed God into my life years ago, but I regret that I did not do it sooner. Embracing His faith has made a tremendous difference in my life and my overall well-being. I pray regularly. I know that God can be a tremendous inspiration through good times and bad. When you are involved in a dangerous sport like auto racing, you rely on a higher power to keep you safe and [help you] overcome adversity. Whether I win or lose a race, I am content with the outcome knowing that I can always trust in God's goodness. We all have to experience our own spiritual journey. But if you embrace God's power, I believe you will live your life with a renewed joy and a heightened sense of fulfillment."

Michael McDowell: Current Sprint Cup and Nationwide Series driver

"I did not grow up in a religious family; I never went to church for anything other than weddings and funerals. When I met my wife Jami, we started spending time with her Uncle Deano and Aunt Kym. They were fun to be around, and they invited us to their church a few times. During this time, I was working hard trying to make it in racing. I had no money, so I spent a lot of time coaching kids and adults in go-karts. I started working for Ron Huber, who was a great man of faith. I always thought he was a very special person who treated his family, friends, and employees with love and integrity. After Ron died, God used his passing to open my heart. Tom Barnett challenged me at Ron's funeral about my life. He asked me if I thought Ron was in heaven, and I obviously said yes. Then he asked me if I was to die today, would I go to heaven. I paused. I really didn't know. A short while later, my wife and I were at church with her aunt and uncle. The pastor was speaking about forgiveness and starting a new life. I thought to myself, *Man that would be nice — a second chance to have all my sins washed away, to be forgiven, and start over.* I prayed that day, that very second. My faith has brought me through a lot of struggles as well as great times of joy and peace."

Kyle Petty: Won eight Sprint Cup races, now a commentator for SPEED and TNT

"There are a lot of people who go to church but never understand the Bible. They are just going through the motions. I think that is where people are living, by the law and not by grace. I grew up going to church with my mother and grandmother. I was going through the motions. I never really realized what was going on — I didn't pick up on having faith in Christ. When I was 15, my uncle was killed in a pit road accident, and I was right there with him. I realized how close I came to being killed. I realized that if I was going to be in this sport, I needed Someone to protect me. You can't do it on your own. I gave my life over to the Lord. Every time I get into a race car, I turn everything over to Him. Unless you build your house on the Rock, Jesus, it's going to fall."

Chapter 13

Moving Through Speedweeks

The deal-making was over. Testing was finished. Now it was time for Sprint Cup Series driver Trevor Bayne and Wood Brothers Racing to see how they stacked up against the competition at NASCAR's most respected racetrack—Daytona International Speedway.

Speedweeks is no ordinary event. Over a three-week span, the track hosts the most prestigious sports car race in America—the Rolex 24 at Daytona—followed by eleven days of stock car racing.

One of those days is devoted to Daytona 500 qualifying. The two cars that post the fastest lap get locked in to the forty-three-car starting grid. Then on the Thursday before the "Great American Race," the track hosts the Gatorade Duel, which is actually two, 150-mile qualifying races that set the rest of the field for the Daytona 500. Sprint Cup teams have from the middle of November

Jeff Gordon (24) and Trevor Bayne (21) compete in the second race of the Gatorade 150 Mile at Daytona International Speedway in Daytona Beach, Florida, Thursday, February 17, 2011.

to the end of January to build and tweak the finest stock cars for this amazing challenge that kicks off the NASCAR season.

Heading into Speedweeks, Trevor showed a lot of confidence as he addressed the media on February 10, 2011.

"I want to be realistic, but I'm also an optimist. So I'm going to say that we're going to be really competitive," Bayne said. "I think setting those high expectations will make us perform better. We have all the equipment. We have the support from Ford Racing.... The Wood brothers have poured their heart and soul into this. You can

Jeff Siner/MCT/Landov

see a lot of excitement going on. They said they haven't felt this excited going into a Sprint Cup racing season in a long time, so to hear that gives me a little boost to see the confidence they already have in me."

Bayne's first official duty in the number 21 Wood Brothers Racing Ford was to post a qualifying speed for the Daytona 500. He had a surprisingly quick run on February 13. For about ten minutes, he was penciled into the front row of the 500 with a qualifying speed of 185.445 mph.

Soon after Bayne's run, Dale Earnhardt Jr. posted the fastest lap at 186.089 mph. Jeff Gordon showed he had plenty left in the tank by nabbing outside pole position honors with a lap clocked at 185.966. But finishing third in time trials at his first Daytona wasn't too bad.

"It was cool," Bayne said. "If I'm gonna get knocked off by somebody, I'm sure the fans were glad it was Dale Jr. But to be sitting third behind two of the most well-known drivers in NASCAR, including Jeff Gordon—my childhood hero—this is incredible."

Bayne added that he was praying a lot before taking his qualifying laps. The winds were calm and the car ran perfectly. With such a fast car, Bayne stayed excited about Thursday's qualifying races.

"We've got an awesome racecar," he said. "Maybe [other drivers] will see that and help us out, so we can get a good starting spot in the 500."

Bayne may have posted the third-quickest speed, but his starting position in the Daytona 500 would depend on how he finished in the second Gatorade Duel.

Bayne was having a great time behind the wheel of the best racecar he had ever driven. But the nineteen-year-old was equally energized by spending time with Gordon. Gordon spent the early days of Speedweeks helping to school Bayne on the tandem racing technique. During the Gatorade Duel qualifying race, they were nearly inseparable. Bayne stayed behind Gordon for most of the race. At one time, Gordon led ten laps with Bayne pushing from behind.

"Jeff Gordon and I worked awesome together, and it was just down there at the end," Bayne said after the race.

On the final lap, all twenty-three cars were gunning it to the finish line to qualify in as high a position as possible. Bayne was high on the track with two cars below him when he ran out of real estate and grazed the wall. Instead of finishing with the leaders, Bayne ended up nineteenth and was credited with running fifty-nine of the sixty laps. Not only did his finish suffer, but the bodywork of his car was dinged up.

"That kind of stinks," Bayne said about the accident. "I hate it for all these guys because we were doing awesome."

Despite the poor finish, many people in Bayne's inner-circle were encouraged by his progress and the

David Ragan (6) and Trevor Bayne (21) crash as Jeff Gordon (24) drives past on the final lap of the second of two qualifying races for Sunday's NASCAR Daytona 500 auto race, at Daytona International Speedway in Daytona Beach, Florida, Thursday, February 17, 2011.

relationships he was making. Bayne's father, Rocky, was especially impressed with Gordon.

"For Jeff Gordon to help Trevor at Daytona is just crazy," Rocky said. "Jeff didn't have to do what he did, because he had nothing to gain in the qualifying race. He stayed out there that whole race; put his car in jeopardy, to work with Trevor."

A lot of the competitors were working extra hard on their driving during 2011 Speedweeks. Daytona International Speedway had been repaved following the 2010 Coke Zero 400. The primary contractor, Lane Construction, pulled up the thirty-two-year-old asphalt and replaced it with four layers of high-tech polymer asphalt cement. The new surface had much more grip than the old, slippery asphalt.

During that same time, the front and rear bumpers of the new stock cars had been redesigned and now lined up like pieces of a jigsaw puzzle.

With the new racing surface and the cars able to "lock up" all the way around the track, tandem racing was born. The drivers quickly discovered that two cars running nose-to-tail were faster than one car—by about ten miles per hour! Two cars were even faster than a line of stock cars, which was normally how races were run—in long lines of cars using an aerodynamic effect called "the draft."

The media called it a "two-car tango." Bayne found that he was really good at pushing the car ahead of him.

"The pushing car is just the engine," Bayne explained.

"The lead car's duties are to make sure to protect the high side, so you don't get unplugged—as we call it."

Bayne made tandem racing sound easy. It isn't. NASCAR greats and past Daytona winners found the new racing style stressful.

Michael Waltrip commented that "pushing" another car is "crazy. You're just so focused," the two-time Daytona winner said. "You're watching your temperature gauge. You're watching the car ahead of you. You're wondering what's up ahead. You're wondering who is catching you from behind. There are just so many things happening mentally, it's almost impossible to keep up."

Following Bayne's accident in the qualifier on Thursday, team owners Eddie and Len Wood had to make a critical decision. Did they want to repair the rumpled number 21 Ford or go to an untested backup car?

With only two days before the race, they decided to fix the car they'd spent most of the winter getting ready for the 500.

"We were standing there looking at the car after the race and some of the guys in Jack's [Roush Fenway Racing] shop who helped build the car to start with said they could fix it," Len Wood said. "They had the parts to do it, so Donnie [Wingo] was trying to weigh out whether we needed practice or not. The decision was made to fix it."

Bayne did not practice at all as the Wood/Roush teams replaced the damaged bodywork. The car was ready on Saturday when Bayne competed in the

Nationwide Series race the day before the Daytona 500. He led that race twice for nine laps before settling on a tenth place finish. With his Sprint Cup car repaired and his confidence high, Bayne felt good about his chances for a top-ten finish in the 500.

Chapter 14

The Golden Moment

When Daytona International Speedway opened its garage gates to NASCAR Sprint Cup Series competitors for 2011 Speedweeks, there was a buzz about the number 21 Wood Brothers Racing Ford and its rookie driver, Trevor Bayne. The Wood family was celebrating its sixtieth year of NASCAR competition and had painted the Ford Fusion in old-school colors— the same colors David Pearson had on the car when he beat Richard Petty.

Insiders knew the number 21 would be a force. Bayne had already proven he could go fast on Dayton's tri-oval. He had flown around the track in December, when he'd done some tire testing for Goodyear Racing. During open testing with Wood Brothers Racing in January, he'd shown a natural ability on the 2.5 mile track. Then during Speedweeks, he'd notched the third fastest qualifying time and done well in the races—except for the accident.

That accident had moved Bayne back in qualifying to the thirty-second spot.

Not only had Bayne's early performances started a buzz, they'd earned him the respect of other NASCAR Sprint Cup drivers. While some people think stock car drivers are daredevils who drive at insane speeds without regard for themselves or their opponents, nothing could be further from the truth.

Sure, NASCAR drivers push themselves and their machines to the limits. But they're not reckless. They don't take unnecessary risks. Respect and trust are important in racing, especially when drivers are inches apart in a high-banked curve going 170 mph.

"It's pretty neat to be going that fast and have confidence in the guy racing beside you," Bobby Labonte said. "Guys aren't going out there to be crazy and stupid. If you take chances, you'll get somebody or yourself hurt. But if you don't go as fast as you can, you won't stay in your ride very long."

Walking that line between driving safely and fast is something that takes drivers years to learn. Bayne seemed to show that ability right from the start.

"He hasn't done anything dumb. That's hard for us drivers sometimes," Carl Edwards said in a 2011 ESPN. com story. Edwards knew Bayne from competing against him during the 2010 Nationwide Series. "He's done a really good job of keeping his composure. He just hasn't made any mistakes.... He drives like a veteran."

And Bayne acted like a veteran from the moment he showed up at the Daytona International Speedway on February 20, 2011.

He attended a church service held inside the garage area, prayed with family and friends, and led a prayer with his team before climbing into the cockpit of his red-and-white stock car trimmed with gold paint.

When the call came to fire up the engines, Bayne was ready. He spent a good part of the race pushing other drivers to the front of the forty-three-car field. He'd pushed a number of different drivers, but had never been in the lead ... until the last two laps.

Just three years before, Bayne was working in the shop at Dale Earnhardt Inc. Now he was on the threshold of NASCAR greatness. He held off all challengers and made a genius move to go low on the track out of turn four to cut off Carl Edwards and earn the checkered flag.

Instead of making a beeline for Victory Lane, Bayne pulled his stock car in front of the main grandstands, climbed out, and stood on the driver's side window with both arms over his head, fists clenched. Bayne was numb after the victory. He couldn't believe it had happened.

Eddie and Len Wood were ecstatic. "Trevor Bayne did such a good job," Eddie said. "To be twenty years old and go fender-to-fender with all these guys ... he's got the composure and savvy of a veteran."

Bayne's composure may have even gone beyond veteran status. Following the race, Edwards said his head hurt, but he wasn't sure if it was from dehydration or stress.

Trevor celebrates winning the Daytona 500 by pulling his car in front of the grandstands instead of making a beeline for Victory Lane.

"That was like 520 miles of sheer terror out there," Edwards said in *The Florida Times-Union* about the extra-long race. "It was just wild. The only reason we didn't wreck more often is because of how good the drivers are, how much patience everyone used, and their discretion with their maneuvering."

The victory was obviously the biggest in Bayne's racing career, but he was quick to point out that winning the Daytona 500 was not the high point of his life.

"The biggest thing I've ever done—and ever could do—is finding Christ," he said. "That's the biggest thing. That's the reason I'm here."

Unlike some athletes who get emotional raising a trophy or talking about a victory, Bayne was very matter-of-fact when he discussed the race. However, when questions turned to his faith in Jesus Christ, the twenty-year-old got a little emotional.

"If it wasn't for [Jesus], there is no way I'd be sitting here," Bayne said. "That gives us purpose. [Victories] are great things, but they go away with time. [A relationship with Christ is] something that can never go away."

In true Christian spirit, Bayne said some of his winnings would go to charity. When asked if he'd splurge on a few luxury items, Bayne had the perfect answer: "I don't know if I will splurge," he said. "I'm definitely not putting it up for retirement. I'm going to stay around for a while."

"I've got a couple of other projects I'm working on to help kids," added Bayne, who lives a somewhat simple lifestyle, sharing an apartment and driving a company car. "I know there are a ton of organizations out there that need help, but I've been [to Mexico]. I was with those kids, so I had that personal experience. You would be surprised what five dollars can do. It can feed a family for a day. It's very cool to be involved with helping people."

Helping people feels good, but sometimes it doesn't feel as good to be on the other side—to be the one who needs help. But Bayne was about to enter a time where he'd call out for the help of others.

Chapter 15

Life as a Champion

For a NASCAR driver, winning the Daytona 500 is like a baseball player hitting a home run to win game seven of the World Series or a wide receiver catching the winning touchdown in the Super Bowl. It's big.

Trevor Bayne knew the fame train was coming. He just wanted to stay humble. The morning after the 500, his parents found a piece of paper in the motor home when they woke up. On the scrap of paper, Trevor had written: "How do I stay grounded in my faith when I'm so high on winning this race? What do I pray for?"

That wasn't the only thing his parents found in the morning. According to the *Florida Times-Union*, more than 15,000 people had joined Trevor's Twitter account in just one hour the night before!

From Monday morning until the next race the following Sunday at Phoenix International Raceway, Bayne was whisked away on a whirlwind media tour. His name and boyish smile appeared everywhere.

Even after racing in Phoenix, Bayne appeared to only get busier. On some weekends, he'd drive in both the Nationwide and Sprint Cup Series. Then during the week, he'd make appearances.

At an autograph signing for Wood Brothers Racing in Stuart, Virginia, at the end of March, Bayne showed up at 6 p.m. for what was supposed to be two hours of interacting with fans. But there were so many fans, Bayne didn't stop signing autographs until well past midnight.

"I'm the kind of person where I don't say no to anything," Bayne told ESPN.com's Marty Smith. "I'll do whatever anybody asks and try to keep every person happy, whether it's a fan on the side of the road, a local newspaper or [the vice president]. I want everybody to have the same experience."

Keeping the balance of being there for the fans and taking time to prepare for races proved to be Bayne's most difficult transition. He always seemed to be on the go. People close to the twenty-year-old were amazed at his energy and stamina.

After reviewing his son's travel itinerary, Rocky was concerned for Trevor. "I'd just like to slow everything down," Rocky said. "Slow it down a little, so he can enjoy the experience more. It's all going so fast."

Such is the go, go, go world of NASCAR. Of course, everything was very exciting for Trevor. He saw each interview and speaking opportunity as a way to spread the truth about God.

Since winning the race, Trevor is constantly surrounded by fans everywhere he goes. Here he signs autographs during qualifying for the STP 300 race at the Chicagoland Speedway in Joliet, Illinois, June 4, 2011.

The Bible says that God sometimes speaks to His people in a whisper. But to hear Him, you have to be still.

Bayne's schedule kept him pretty frantic ... until April 23, 2011. After finishing sixth in the Nationwide Series race at Nashville Superspeedway, the young driver sat out the next five weeks of competition due to double vision.

The symptoms started the previous week at Talladega, when Bayne climbed out of the Roush Fenway car feeling fatigued and nauseous. At first he thought he was just a little rundown. Doctors thought the reaction could be due to a bug bite he'd suffered earlier in the month.

At first Bayne believed he could just power through the feelings of weakness, but then he started to get double vision.

"I was out hiking [on Monday] at a place called Midnight Hole," Bayne said. "It's in North Carolina near the Tennessee line. We were hiking and jumping off waterfalls. My eyes were perfect."

Bayne went to bed, feeling fine. He woke up Tuesday and his eyes couldn't focus. He had to do a radio show, so he kept his eyes closed while talking on the phone. Bayne went back to bed, hoping a little more sleep would help. But when he woke up an hour later, he felt like he'd gone cross-eyed.

"I went to look in the mirror, and I couldn't see myself," Bayne said. "I woke up my friend and I asked him, 'Am I cross-eyed right now?' He told me, 'No, you look fine.'"

At this point, Bayne wasn't freaking out, but he knew he had to see a doctor. The eye doctor said he had double vision, so he went to the mall to try on corrective glasses. Nothing worked. Bayne went to the hospital that night and then transferred to one of the best hospitals in the country—the Mayo Clinic in Rochester, Minnesota—to be diagnosed and treated.

A team of doctors tested for every illness, disease, and ailment that carried his symptoms. All the tests were negative. He stayed at the Mayo Clinic for nearly two weeks.

"They didn't know what the problem was, but they treated me for a couple of things [including Lyme disease]," Bayne said. "They didn't know how fast I would get better. I wore an eye patch every day, because if I didn't I would get sick to my stomach."

When a driver can't race, it affects a lot of people. His crew, his sponsors, the car owner. At the time Bayne went into the hospital, he was fifth in Nationwide Series points. But nobody was thinking about a run at the Nationwide title. They all just wanted to see the young driver back on his feet again.

The NASCAR community rallied around Bayne. Tony Stewart sent his private jet to Knoxville to pick up Trevor's mother and younger siblings so they could visit him at Mayo.

"I got there, and he had a patch over one eye and looked like a little pirate," Stephanie said. "I'm sitting there, looking at him, being worried and he said, 'You know, everybody is looking at me so stressed out and worried. You need to stop, because I'm not worried. God knows what he's doing.'"

NASCAR driver Carl Edwards dropped by Bayne's room to play his guitar and sing a few songs. Michael McDowell stayed all week, and his family visited, too. Brent Weaver came out for a day and stayed with Bayne during his time in the hospital.

After a few weeks, Bayne felt well enough to go home. Doctors still didn't know what had caused the blurred vision, but they'd done everything for him that they could.

"After the third day back in Knoxville, I could finally take that patch off again," Bayne said. "That's when I started making a fast recovery. After about a week out of the hospital, I felt like I was almost back to 100 percent."

In the short span of three months, Bayne had topped the highest mountain and fallen into the deepest valley. Through it all, he had a peace that he couldn't explain, but that impressed the people around him.

"I've heard him say several times, 'If winning the Daytona 500 was the moment that defined me, it would be horrible to go from that high to that low. It's my faith in Jesus that defines me,'" Stephanie said. "I'm in awe when he says things like that, I'm thinking, *How does he know that? He's only twenty years old.*"

Doctors cleared Bayne to race again at the STP 300 at the Chicagoland Speedway in the beginning of June. He didn't know what had made him feel so miserable for over a month, but he did know he was happy to be back behind the wheel.

"This has probably been the toughest five weeks that I've experienced," Bayne said before the Nationwide Series race. "At the same time, it's been a good five weeks, because I realized how lucky I am to drive a race-car every weekend."

And once Bayne got behind the wheel in Chicago, race fans realized how lucky they were to be able to watch him.

Chapter 16

Back on Track

Racecar drivers race. It's that simple. And Trevor Bayne is a racecar driver. Being away from the track for a month and a half didn't diminish Bayne's skills at all. In fact, from the way he drove at the STP 300 on June 4, 2011, the layoff had only made him hungrier.

Bayne announced he was back the night before the race by recording the fastest speed at happy hour, topping out at 174.081 mph.

During the Nationwide event, Bayne drove with the skill and calmness that earned him a Sprint Cup Series ride when he was only nineteen. Justin Allgaier won the race by passing Carl Edwards on the backstretch of the final lap when Edwards ran out of gas. Allgaier also ran out of gas, but coasted across the line for the victory. If the race would have been a little longer, Bayne could have won. He placed third.

Throughout the summer, Bayne continued to have success in the Nationwide series. Two weeks after returning in Chicago, Bayne scored his second-consecutive top-five finish by placing fifth at the Michigan International Speedway.

Bayne returned to Daytona International Speedway at the beginning of July to compete in the Sprint Cup Coke Zero 400. Again, he showed he could drive fast on the track by qualifying second. But just four laps into the race, Bayne got bumped and crashed into the wall. Damage to his number 21 Ford forced him to drop out of the race. David Ragan, who had gotten black-flagged during the Daytona 500, redeemed himself in Daytona by winning the race.

Even though Bayne was racing every weekend, he still got questions about the ailment that kept him off the track all of May. Bayne didn't mind the questions. He just wanted to prove that he was totally back.

"I finally just had to accept that nobody knows," Bayne said when asked about his mysterious illness. "I can promise that if I was just tired or not feeling great, I would have still been in the racecar, because I am a racer."

As soon as Bayne started racing again, his life resumed its blur of activity. He did take a weekend off in the beginning of July to relax. But he was back at it the next week as he flew to Los Angeles to attend the ESPN Awards on July 13. Bayne had been nominated for "Best Sport Moment" of the year.

Scott A. Miller/AP Images

Trevor hangs out during qualifying for the Coke Zero 400 at Daytona International Speedway on July 1, 2011 in Daytona Beach, Florida.

Although he didn't end up winning (the award went to Philadelphia Phillies pitcher Roy Halladay for his no-hitter in the playoffs), Bayne enjoyed seeing many of the world's best athletes.

"Our red carpet experience was a whole different world for me," Bayne wrote in his blog for *USA Today*. "I had never seen that many celebrities in that close quarters. I did so many interviews and smiled so much for pictures it was exhausting."

Exhausting and exhilarating. "I rubbed elbows with so many athletes I had admired over the years," he added. "At one point, I had to ask myself if this was really happening."

Right after the show, Bayne said his goodbyes and caught a red-eye flight to Boston. He had to be at Fenway Park for an ESPN feature about himself and Roush Fenway Racing driver Ricky Stenhouse Jr. Then on Friday, he was the keynote speaker for the annual New Hampshire Governor's breakfast at the New Hampshire Motor Speedway.

During the New England 200 on Saturday, Bayne led for fifty-eight laps. Several cautions and a wreck caused him to drop back some. But he still finished a respectable thirteenth.

Watching Bayne drive, it's obvious that his best racing is still ahead of him. And the people on his team agree. Jamie Allison, the head of Ford Racing, is completely sold on the whole Trevor Bayne package.

"When Trevor was going through what he was going through with his eyes, you learn a lot about people during their difficult moments," Allison said. "I tell you, this kid continues to impress me. He has wisdom beyond his age." As Allison expressed, we all know that life will throw us a lot of different stuff, whether on the racetrack or off, and Trevor has a maturity that compliments his skills. "I expect Trevor to be a star in this sport for many years to come."

Jack Roush, who knows a little something about driving after winning thirty-two championships and 400 competitions in drag racing, sports cars, and stock cars, believes Bayne is the real deal.

"He came back like gangbusters when he was able to get back in the car," Roush said. "Trevor Bayne is going to be in this business for a long time."

That's Bayne's hope, too. Through a majority of the 2011 Nationwide Series, he claimed eight top-ten finishes and three top-fives in seventeen starts. He also placed sixteenth at Michigan International Speedway—his top Sprint Cup finish after winning Daytona.

"He has tremendous awareness in the car," Wood said in an ESPN.com story. "The great ones are like that. And he will be a great one."

No matter what happens in the future, Bayne and NASCAR fans around the world will never forget his wild ride in 2011.

"This year has been really crazy—going from winning the Daytona 500 to being in the hospital," Bayne said. "Hopefully, we'll have some more highs. It's been a really good story to watch unfold."

And this young driver knows that God will continue to write his story in the years to come.

"My faith in God is the biggest thing," he said. "I know it's all part of the plan for me. I just have to keep peace in that."

Acknowledgments

A big thank you to all who helped me complete this book. Trevor Bayne, Stephanie Bayne, Rocky Bayne, Brent Weaver, Michael McDowell, Jimmie Johnson, Jack Roush, Kim Childress, Annette Bourland, and Danielle Randall-Bauer. A special "thanks buddy" to Scott Sterbens, who took time away from his busy schedule, and his son Trevor, to lend his editing wisdom to the project.